72 Things Younger

Than John McCain

Joe Quint

A Fireside Book

Published by Simon & Schuster

NEW YORK LONDON TORONTO SYDNEY

Fireside
A Division of Simon & Schuster, Inc.
1230 Avenue of the Americas
New York, NY 10020

First Fireside trade paperback edition August 2008

FIRESIDE and colophon are registered trademarks of Simon & Schuster, Inc.

For information about special discounts for bulk purchases, please contact Simon & Schuster Special Sales
at 1-800-456-6798 or business@simonandschuster.com.

Designed by Timothy Shaner, nightanddaydesign.biz

Manufactured in the United States of America

10 9 8 7 6 5 4 3 2 1

ISBN-13: 978-1-4391-0227-5
ISBN-10:   1-4391-0227-9

To Suzanne, for listening to me ramble on about politics for fifteen years. Here's to fifty more.

John Sidney McCain III,
born August 29, 1936

Introduction

Back in April 2008, a friend and I took a road trip to Philadelphia to do some volunteer work for the Obama campaign. While the primary results would later prove that we didn't work nearly hard enough, the trip wasn't a total loss, as we did end up having a great conversation about the nonsense that the so-called pundits of the mainstream media were, once again, trying to turn into campaign issues—things like lapel pins with little flags on them, bowling scores, and the comments made by a candidate's former pastor . . . while the real issues of the day were, as usual, getting little more than lip service.

But fine—this is what the media does. It then begged the question of why no one was talking seriously about the issue of potentially electing our oldest president ever during what might very well be one of the most complicated and critical periods in our history.

"This matters," we said over cheesesteaks and Dr. Brown's Black Cherry soda at Jim's Steaks (4th and South streets and, incidentally, younger than John McCain), "and not because I like young people more than I like old people, but because all experience isn't necessarily good experience and because it's important to be relevant, inspiring, exciting, engaging, and sharp."

So a list of things younger than John McCain was born— starting with Ronald Reagan (who was younger at the time of his inauguration than McCain would be at his) and including the polio vaccine, AARP, FM radio, McDonald's, and a whole host of other things that are deeply ingrained in our way of life. I feel that, by picking ubiquitous products, items from popular culture, famous people that seem older than McCain but really aren't (paging Keith Richards . . .), I'm able to both hammer home the idea of how age (unlike gender or race) could impact the effectiveness and success of a president and also have some fun at the same time.

72 Things Younger Than John McCain

Ronald Reagan

At the time of his inauguration, Ronald Reagan was a spritely 69 years, 11 months, and 17 days old. He was known to be big on naps.

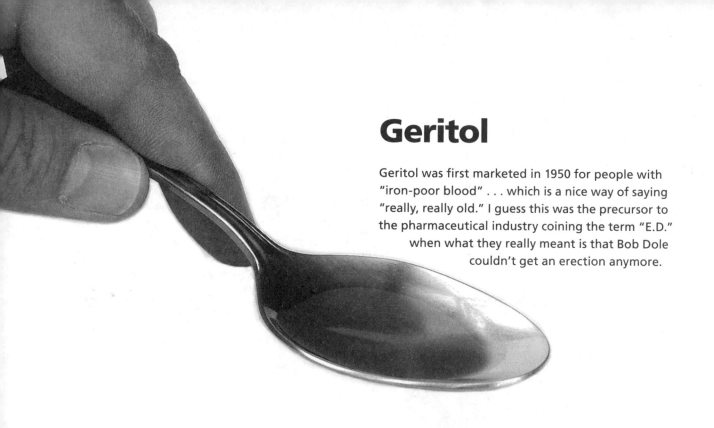

Geritol

Geritol was first marketed in 1950 for people with "iron-poor blood" . . . which is a nice way of saying "really, really old." I guess this was the precursor to the pharmaceutical industry coining the term "E.D." when what they really meant is that Bob Dole couldn't get an erection anymore.

The Jefferson Memorial

Much like the pyramids in Egypt, Stonehenge, the moai on Easter Island, and the mystery liquid found rain or shine on the sidewalks of New York City, I always thought that the presidential monuments were things that had always been on the landscape. I was shocked—shocked, I say—to learn that the one to Thomas Jefferson was dedicated seven years after John McCain was born.

As I always get the monuments confused, I came up with a simple way to distinguish them: the Jefferson Memorial is the one that doesn't look like either Lincoln or a giant penis.

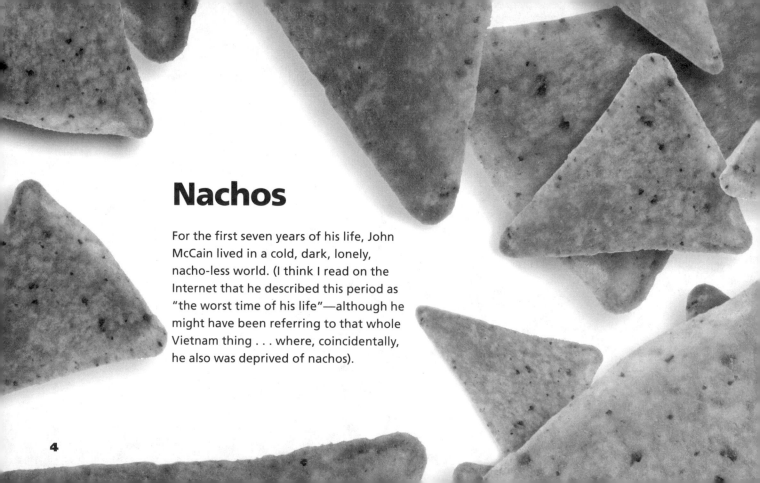

Nachos

For the first seven years of his life, John McCain lived in a cold, dark, lonely, nacho-less world. (I think I read on the Internet that he described this period as "the worst time of his life"—although he might have been referring to that whole Vietnam thing . . . where, coincidentally, he also was deprived of nachos).

The Hobbit

Let me start out by saying that the only thing I know about *The Hobbit* is that it was published in 1937. Other than that, nada. I never read it, I never saw any of the movies, I wouldn't know Middle-Earth from a hole in the ground, and I can't stand *Monty Python*  (it seems to me that people who like *The Hobbit* and *Lord of the Rings* often also like *Monty Python*).

Here's another thing I know—*The Hobbit* is a really, really old book.

And John McCain is older.

Ed Bradley

I've always liked the late Ed Bradley. Maybe it was the earring and how he tried to be the "cool" *60 Minutes* reporter—or maybe it was because listening to Andy Rooney drone on and on about his shoelaces made me want to set myself on fire— but I always thought he seemed like a decent guy.

Probably would have been too old to be president, but a decent guy nonetheless.

Oklahoma!

No, not the state (the state was established an amazingly short 29 years before McCain was born!), but the first collaboration of Rodgers and Hammerstein.

"Flesh"-colored Crayola Crayons

I could be wrong, but I think I remember seeing a filmstrip in elementary school that showed cavemen writing on walls with Crayola crayons. Actually, the truth is that the bulk of the colors in the current rotation appeared in the fancy box, with the sharpener in back, in the late 1940s.

Interestingly enough, the color name "Flesh" was changed to "Peach" in the 1960s due in large part to the U.S. civil rights movement . . . because, you know, there's more than one color of flesh.

This Car

This is what cars looked like in the year John McCain was born. They probably did zero to sixty in a few minutes and got five gallons to the mile.

Turn Signals

Speaking of ancient cars, when Ma and Pa McCain were driving little Johnny to and from what I'm sure was a lovely and kid-friendly daycare center in the barracks of the military base where he was born, they didn't use "directionals"—presumably, they stuck an arm out the window and hoped that the guy behind them know that tilting your arm up at an angle means that you want to make a right.

I guess it didn't matter all that much that turn signals weren't available on consumer cars until 1939—as the Interstate Highway System had yet to be adopted.

The Paint Roller

1940 was a big year for the advancement of painting. It seems that one Norman James Breakey of Canada invented the basic design of the paint roller . . . only to have Richard Croxton Adams get the patent. And the girls.

Rice-A-Roni

You gotta love marketing folks. They can make something as bland, lifeless, and painfully dull as rice sound exciting simply by adding "A-Roni" to the end of it. Doesn't that make you hungry for rice? Don't you just want to run out and buy some rice RIGHT NOW?

    Note to McCain's campaign manager: Try "McCain-A-Roni in '08" on for size.

The Phillips Screw

Aaahh—what a simple time it was when John McCain was born. If you were working with a friend to install, for example, a fluorescent light fixture (no, wait—those weren't introduced until 1937 . . . well, let's just pretend they were available), and he asked for a screwdriver, you didn't have to slow down progress by asking, "Which kind—Phillips or regular?"

Good times. Good, old, ancient times.

(Okay, I know that technically the Phillips screw was patented about a month before McCain was born—but I'm assuming that they didn't reach the screw-using public until sometime later. Go with it.)

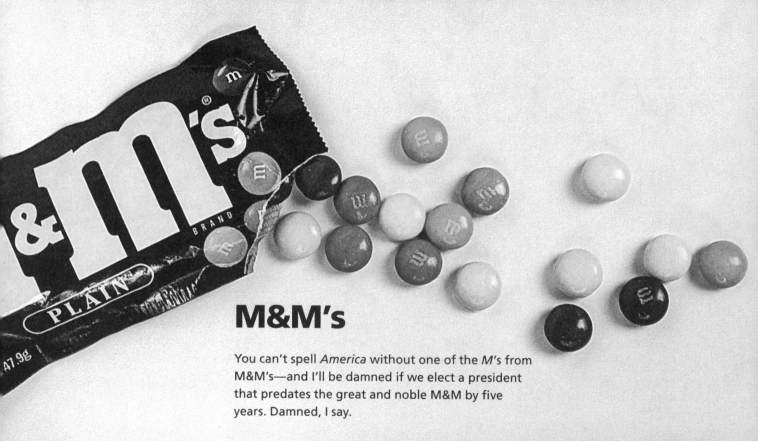

M&M's

You can't spell *America* without one of the *M*'s from M&M's—and I'll be damned if we elect a president that predates the great and noble M&M by five years. Damned, I say.

Two-ply Toilet Paper

In the year before John McCain was born, the Northern Tissue Paper Company proudly proclaimed its toilet paper to be "splinter free"—but it wasn't until John McCain had been out of diapers for about four years that the world was treated to the miracle of a second layer of paper.

Latex Paint

Younger and only slightly less interesting
than John McCain.

Rice Krispies Treats

I was never a huge fan of the Rice Krispies Treats (invented in 1939) . . . largely because, as I've told my wife time and again, Jews don't like to eat with their hands. At least this Jew doesn't. Corn on the cob? No thanks. Baklava? Not for me. I'll make the (very) occasional exception for spare ribs from the Empire Szechuan on Greenwich Avenue and, of course, burgers and hot dogs are exempt, but other than that it's a pretty black-and-white thing.

But I digress. John McCain is really old.

Roll-On Antiperspirant

The world was a much sweatier place when John McCain was born.

Roll-on antiperspirant, modeled after the ballpoint pen technology, didn't become available until the 1950s.

The Ten Commandments

See that *The Ten Commandments* is in italic? It's because I'm referring to the movie starring late gun nut Charlton Heston and not the tablets themselves (although I fact-checked those, too, just to make sure).

Much like *Goodfellas*, *The Godfather* (parts I and II, not III), and *Lost in America*, this is one of those movies that I never tire of watching. When Moses says "Get your stinking paws off me, you damn dirty apes," I always stand up and cheer, "You tell 'em, Moses! Let your people go!"

The 22nd Amendment

I have a lot of favorite amendments. Speech is a good one, as are the ones about cruel and unusual punishment, due process, and the abolition of slavery. But these days I'm particularly fond of good ol' 22—because that's the one that says the George W. Bush can't run again.

I guess it's something of a moot point when it comes to John McCain—because, if he were to win, he would almost certainly be a one-term president (which, while being very good for the country, would be very bad for book sales).

Oyster Pails

I don't know what people did with their leftover Chinese food in the days of John McCain's youth—and, being of weak stomach, I don't really care to know. What I do know is that were it not for these little white boxes of joy, my refrigerator (prewife—had to get that in there) would contain nothing but club soda and a lightbulb.

The Nylon-Bristle Toothbrush

John McCain seemingly has good choppers. As does Barack Obama. And what do they have to thank? Why, the toothbrush—voted history's most important invention in a 2003 poll.

While ancient civilizations used a "chew stick" to brush what they considered to be their teeth, and people did use boar-bristle brushes up until the late 1930s, the modern toothbrush didn't come into existence until the invention of nylon (which is mentioned on page 56—see how everything comes full circle?).

Life

If there was ever a ubiquitous brand—one that seemingly has been on the landscape forever—it's *Life* magazine.

While the original *Life* was born in 1883, the *Life* magazine as we know it was created by Henry Luce (chairman of Time Inc.) in the year that John McCain was born.

Coverage of major (and minor) national events, countless photographs (by the world's most renowned pho-

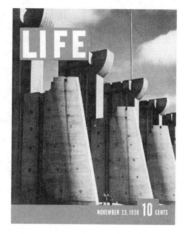

tographers) that are etched into our collective consciousness, ground-breaking journalism—it's all been in *Life*. Before we began to be bombarded daily by media influences on all sides, *Life* was the go-to source for trusted and reliable information in often uncertain times.

(Okay, *Life*, can I get my check now?)

Tom Jones

There was a rumor floating around the Internet in early 2008 that Tom Jones had insured his chest hair with Lloyd's of London for $7 million.

Turns out that, much like most of what you read on the Internet, the rumor was false.

Social Security

The Social Security Act was drafted by President Roosevelt and enacted by Congress as part of the New Deal—but it wasn't until 1937 that payroll taxes were first collected and benefits first paid (specifically, the lump-sum death benefit to over fifty thousand beneficiaries). The first regular monthly payment was made to one Ida May Fuller in 1940.

Here is an excerpt of John McCain's position on Social Security—taken from johnmccain.com:

John McCain will fight to save the future of Social Security and believes that we may meet our obligations to the retirees of today and the future without raising taxes. John McCain supports supplementing the current Social Security system with personal accounts—but not as a substitute for addressing benefit promises that cannot be kept.

So he's going to fix it without raising taxes and he supports privatization sometimes?

Thanks for clarifying. Makes all the sense in the world.

Veterans Day as a National Holiday

In 1919, President Wilson first proclaimed November 11 "Armistice Day" to commemorate the anniversary of the end of World War I—but it wasn't until 1938 that Congress approved an act that set aside the date as a legal holiday. An amendment to the act that came some years later officially changed the name of the holiday to Veterans Day.

Not being a veteran, I always remember the date of Veterans Day because it's the same day as my grandmother's birthday. She lived to be more than 100 and, despite the fact that she was sharp as a tack until about three weeks before she died, I still would have had reservations about her calling the shots in the White House Situation Room.

Don Imus

My issue with Don Imus isn't that, in an attempt to be the poor man's Howard Stern, he made some allegedly racist comments—no, my issue with him has always been that he's just not funny.

And that he looks like a ghost.

The Margarita

The origin of the margarita is a subject of heated debate (well, at least among the five or six people who lay claim to its invention), but my favorite has to be that it was created by Enrique Bastate Gutierrez in the early 1940s as an homage to Rita Hayworth, whose real name was Margarita Cansino ("Cansino" being Spanish for "drink until you can't feel anything from the waist down").

By Law, Many Federal Employees

According to the U.S. Office of Personnel Management, Title 29 of U.S.C. Section 633a states that agencies are [permitted] to establish a maximum age requirement only in instances where they have proven to the Equal Employment Opportunity Commission that age is a bona fide occupational qualification necessary for the performance of the duties of a particular position."

Um, okay—I can think of such a position.

The Zip Code

There are two things I find funny about the fact that John McCain is older than the zip code system:

1. John McCain's first address was something like:

> The Parents of the Oldest Guy Ever
> to Potentially Become President
> 123 Main Street
> East Nowhere 12, VA

Two digits. The country was so damn small back then that there were only two digits in the postal code.

2. It was a postal inspector who submitted a proposal for an updated system in 1944.

When I go to the post office, I'm lucky if I can find someone who isn't breathing through a tube—but apparently, in 1944, postal workers were so motivated by what they were doing that they put in overtime developing new systems for delivering mail. (It should be noted, however, that this system wasn't implemented until the 1960s and, even then, it wasn't mandatory . . . thus restoring my faith in their ineptitude.)

Duct Tape

I've noticed in my travels that a lot of people refer to duct tape as "duck tape"... which is mildly comforting, as that's what I always thought it was called (or, at least, should be called).

Duct tape, duck tape, tomato, tomahto... it seems that this household staple has been around forever—and it has. It's just that John McCain has been around forever-er.

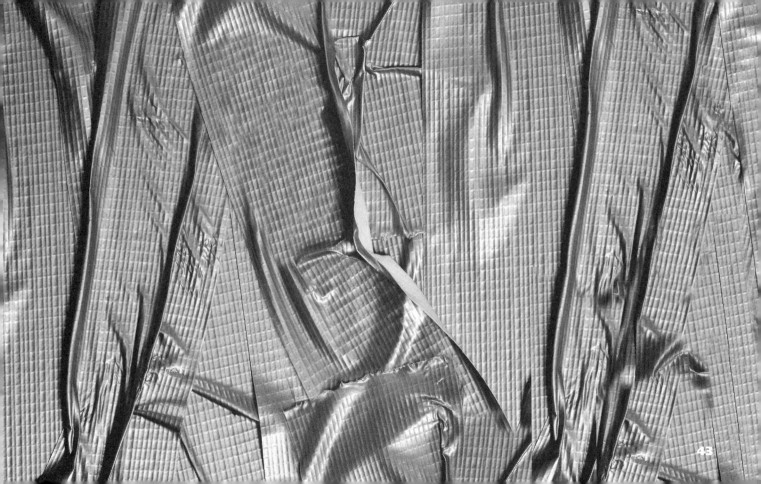
43

43

The 12 Steps of Alcoholics Anonymous

In 1938, a man known as "Bill W." (no *genetic* relationship to George W.) was chosen by about a hundred of his fellow alcoholics to publish a book that promoted their program and included a list of suggested activities (or "steps") for spiritual growth and deliverance from the grip that alcohol held on their lives.

How to Win Friends and Influence People

This classic book by famed deli owner Dale Carnegie (Wait!—What? He wasn't the deli guy? Damn you, Wikipedia!) has enhanced the careers of countless numbers of real estate brokers, used-car salesman, and politicians.

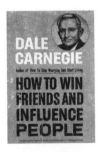

    I shouldn't mock. How can you make fun of a book whose chief principles call for "smiling" and "emphatically admitting when you're wrong"?

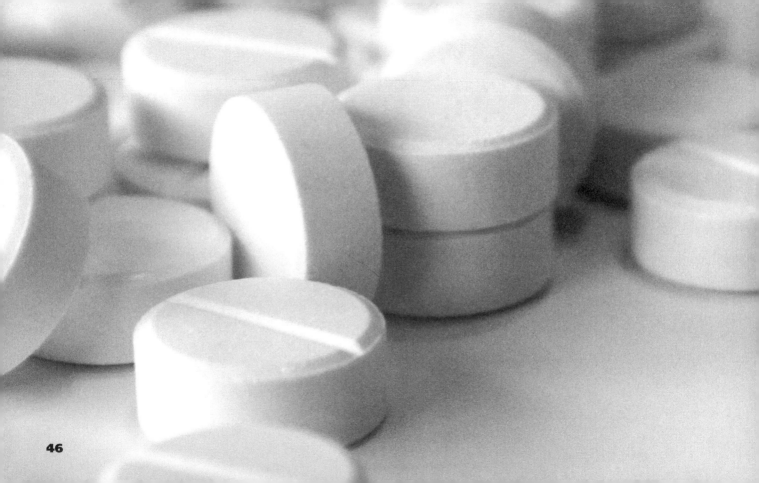

Penicillin

In 1942, when John McCain was presumably an unvaccinated six-year-old, John Bumstead and Orvan Hess became the first physicians in the world to successfully treat a patient using penicillin. At the time, they could not possibly comprehend what this breakthrough would mean for children, soldiers, and generations of Hollywood starlets.

Kraft Macaroni & Cheese

I put Kraft Macaroni & Cheese right up there with the wheel and the iPhone as one of the world's great inventions. Created by divine inspiration in 1937, it's the perfect meal when you have a cold or when you're too lazy to make, you know, real food. The key, however, lies in my own secret technique . . . which I will share with you here and now:

The Double Drain™

You see, the directions call for the chef to drain the water after the macaroni has come to a boil . . . but that's insane. Between the milk, the butter, and the excess water that didn't drain, you'll still be left with a runny mess that will deprive you of the full "cheese" experience. One must do a second, "cleansing" drain just prior to emptying the contents onto ones plate. And one must also use a wooden spoon.

For the less industrious among us, there's a product called Kraft Easy Mac which can be prepared with just water and a microwave in $3^1/_2$ minutes . . . but that's just sad.

Finally, to borrow from a comment that a visitor to my blog wrote about the corn dog (which was one of the five most impassioned odes to the corn dog I've ever read), "Elect a president that was born before the invention of Kraft Macaroni & Cheese? Not on my watch, pal."

The Minimum Wage

This one's a little ambiguous—there were various pieces of legislation setting a minimum wage prior to 1936, but they were all overturned (I guess 25 cents an hour for backbreaking work in a factory was crazy talk back then) . . . but it was reestablished in 1938 by the Fair Labor Standards Act. And this time it stuck.

Since then, the federal minimum wage has skyrocketed to $6.55—which means that, according to our government, someone who earns a pretax paycheck of $262.00 for a forty-hour week is doing just fine.

My Mother

Here's an e-mail I received from my mother after my blog went live:

> I am younger than John McCain and I get senior citizen discounts, I can't bend, my knees hurt, and I just went on Medicare! And, PS, the type on your blog is too small.

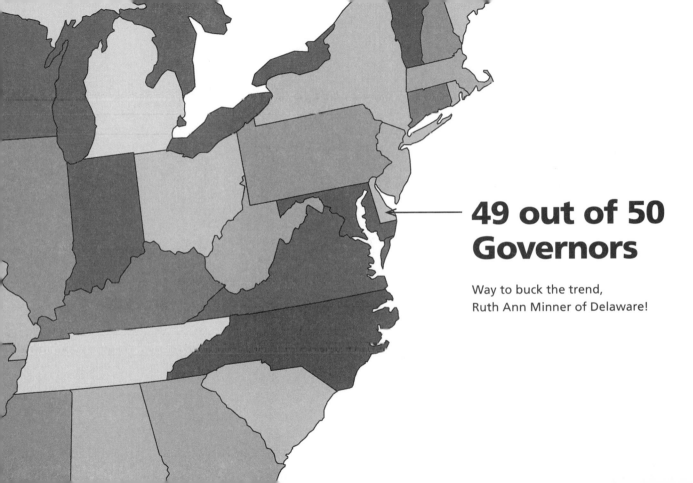

49 out of 50 Governors

Way to buck the trend,
Ruth Ann Minner of Delaware!

Scrabble

How fortuitous. What might very well be the world's best cure for insomnia is actually younger than the man who might very well be the Senate's best cure for insomnia (although there certainly are some quality contenders in that field).

Nylon

Nylon was first used commercially in a nylon-bristle toothbrush in 1938—which makes me wonder what Ma and Pa McCain were using until then to brush little Johnny's first teeth.

Defibrillation (on People)

While defibrillation had been used on animals since 1899, the first use of it on an actual person was when John McCain was in (roughly) the sixth grade.

This photo (left) is an approximation of what I might look like if this old nut becomes president.

Area Codes

While the telephone itself was invented a mere 60 years prior to Pa McCain looking at John and saying to Ma McCain "Some day this boy won't become president," the area code wasn't introduced until the 1940s.

The Shopping Cart

This seems like something cavemen should have invented (which reminds me, I hate those stupid Geico commercials)—I mean, it's wheels and a bucket. It couldn't be simpler. So simple, in fact, that one would think that it not only predates John McCain but that it would predate his parents and grandparents as well.

One would be wrong.

Velcro

As chance would have it, we (the Velcro-loving population) just celebrated the 50th anniversary of the invention of Velcro. Happy birthday, Velcro—and good job keeping John McCain's shoes closed. (You see, because he's old and may have trouble with laces. Get it? *Get it?*)

The Cobb Salad

Contrary to what the guy in the wheelchair said in that episode of *Curb Your Enthusiasm*, the Cobb salad was in fact first created in 1937 by Brown Derby restaurant owner Bob Cobb . . . a point that Larry made abundantly clear.

Cheerios

I have young twins at home and, as any parent will tell you, these little round treasures of toasted whole-grain goodness might as well be called "Crackios" or "Crystal Methios." There's nothing my kids like more than to take a fistful of these suckers and get (maybe) one or two right in their mouths.

I look forward to telling them, come November 2008, that our country had the good sense to elect a president younger than this ubiquitous brand.

And I imagine that they'll poop in celebration.

The Grapes of Wrath

I have to admit that I never read the book and was only turned on to the movie because of the Springsteen album (*The Ghost of Tom Joad*), but its message is timeless.

In a nutshell, the economy was down the drain, lenders were foreclosing left and right, there were more applicants than there were jobs, and people were in search of a way to restore their dignity.

Hmm, I wonder if they'll ever make a sequel?

Spam

The inexpensive lunch meat, as opposed to the Internet nuisance promising greater manhood and hot encounters with stay-at-home moms (which, for the record, this writer has yet to see bear fruit), might likely become a necessary diet of many should this old geezer become president.

The Golden Gate Bridge

Completed in 1937, the Golden Gate Bridge has the longest suspension bridge main span in the United States, after the Verrazano-Narrows Bridge in New York City (which, incidentally, was completed when McCain was in his late twenties).

Chocolate Chip Cookies

Okay, this is an odd one. Apparently, the chocolate chip cookie has not been around since the dawn of time. It did not evolve from anything, nor was it hanging down from the forbidden tree (or whatever it's called) in the Garden of Eden. It was, in fact, invented in 1937 by Ruth Graves Wakefield of Whitman, Massachusetts, who ran the Toll House restaurant.

So this classic staple and friend of milk lovers everywhere is actually younger than John McCain.

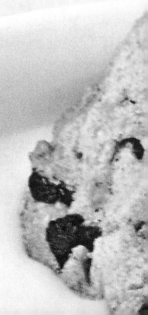

Alaska

Alaska—a whole freaking state—is younger than
John McCain. And so, for that matter, is Hawaii.
McCain is older than two of the fifty states.
This reminds me of one of my all-time favorite jokes:

A polar bear asks his Mother, "Mom, am I a real
polar bear?"
"Yes, darling, of course you are," his mother
answered.
"Are you sure I'm a polar bear?"
"Yes, dear," his mother replied. "You are, I am,
your sister is, your father is. We're all polar bears."
"Are you positive?"
"Yes, yes, for the last time, you're a polar bear!
Why do you keep asking?"
"Because I'm freezing my ass off!"

Anyway, that has nothing to do with John McCain.
But again, this guy is really, really old.

The Slinky

"It's Slinky, it's Slinky,
   for fun it's a wonderful toy.
It's Slinky, it's Slinky,
   it's fun for a girl and a boy."

Before the Slinky, kids played with
rocks and sticks. And before that,
John McCain was born.

Kodachrome

According to the Kodak website, the popular slide film (made even more popular by the classic Paul Simon song—who, incidentally, is way younger than John McCain) can now only be processed at one remaining location in the world: Dwayne's Photo, in Parsons, Kansas.

In other words, Kodachrome, which is younger than John McCain, is almost dead.

Pat Buchanan

Here are some dumb things Pat Buchanan has said:

"Who are beneficiaries of the court's protection? Members of various minorities including criminals, atheists, homosexuals, flag burners, illegal immigrants (including terrorists), convicts, and pornographers."

"Our culture is superior. Our culture is superior because our religion is Christianity and that is the truth that makes men free."

"I think a real problem America has is we've taken this idea of equality and extended it so beyond where it belongs. All lifestyles are not equal. Some are wrong."

And one smart one:

"McCain will make Cheney look like Gandhi."

Not bad for a seventy-year-old.

Scientology

Now, I'm not going to get into whether Scientology is or isn't a religion. You want to believe? Believe. Makes no difference to me. But I will say that most religions I can think of are really old . . . and yet, can you guess who's older?

Here's a hint: It rhymes with Lon McBain.

Plutonium

Plutonium is a rare, radioactive element that was first isolated and produced in 1940. It's a fissile element that's used in most modern nuclear weapons.

Why do I bring this up?

Well, given that much of John McCain's foreign policy proposals seem to indicate that his presidency will deal with North Korea's nuclear program much in the same way Bush did, it would probably be a good idea if we all had a strong working knowledge of plutonium.

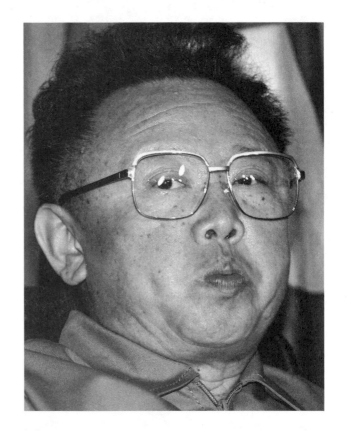

Bugs Bunny

When Elmer Fudd (also younger than McCain), Daffy Duck (younger), or Wile E. Coyote (take a guess) pushed Bugs past his breaking point, he invoked Groucho Marx and uttered the classic line: "Of course you realize, this means war!"

If McCain came out tomorrow and said that this was how he intended to talk to Kim Jong-Il, I'd probably vote for him. (Nah, who am I kidding? I'm not voting for him.)

Jerry Mathers as the Beaver

Contrary to popular opinion, Jerry Mathers was not killed in Vietnam.

And while we're on the subject, Mikey—of Life cereal fame—did not die from mixing Pop Rocks and soda, Microsoft and AOL are not giving away money, Jamie Lee Curtis is not a hermaphrodite, and John McCain didn't lie about his age when he was courting Cindy.

Oh wait, scratch that last one.

AARP

Here's a riddle:

What do AARP and KFC have in common?

They're both organizations that ignore one of the letters in their namesake acronym. (AARP no longer wants to be just for "retired" persons and KFC would rather you not think about their food being "fried".)

Another thing they have in common?

They're both younger than John McCain.

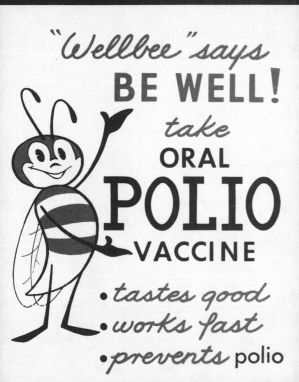

Polio Vaccine

Yeah, there's not really a whole lot of funny things to write about polio. Let's just say McCain is older than the vaccine and move on.

McDonald's

McDonald's is the *Life* magazine of junk food—they've been around so long that it's hard for anyone (except John McCain) to imagine life without those Golden Arches and the intoxicating smell of their french fries.

Here's a random fact about McDonald's:

Willard Scott—friend to centenarians everywhere—claims to have created the Ronald McDonald character in a series of commercials for a McDonald's franchisee. (Oddly, he also played Bozo the clown.)

Israel

Israel turns sixty this year. It's a country. A whole country. And it's younger than the guy who wants to be president of ours.

Dick Cheney

Dick Cheney will not be running for president this year because the Constitution says that you can only be president for two terms.

And besides, he's too old.

Mount Rushmore

Now here's a conundrum: Do I make a "What a coincidence—that mountain looks like a bunch of famous presidents!" joke, a comment about the odd juxtaposition of our current "leader" in front of all those real leaders, or do I just take a cheap shot about which Dakota Rushmore is in (I always forget—because I don't really care)?

The Hindenburg Disaster

Oh the humanity, indeed.

Keith Richards

Craggy-faced Stone Keith Richards is
younger than John McCain.
   Yep, he was born in '43. 1943.

Superman

Whether you know him as "The Man of Steel," "The Last Son of Krypton," or the guy who guest-starred on that episode of *I Love Lucy*, he is younger than presidential hopeful John McCain.

And he can see through things.

This is Helvetica.
It's a sans serif font whose name is derived from the Latin word for Switzerland.

Helvetica

One of our more ubiquitous typefaces, Helvetica is a sans serif font designed when John McCain was in his early twenties. (Incidentally, McCain uses Optima for his campaign materials . . . a typeface that is widely viewed as the ultimate "noncommittal" type-face because it's not really a serif font and it's not really a sans serif font.)

The Ballpoint Pen

While there were prototype ballpoint pens in the era known as BJMC (before John McCain), it wasn't until 1938 that a Hungarian newspaper editor solved the flow problems that were plaguing his predecessors and had his smudge-free name written in the annals of pen history.

The First FM Radio Station

Let me say for the record—without being boastful—that I consider myself a fairly bright guy. I went to a good school, got respectable grades. I can usually do the *New York Times* crossword puzzle up until Wednesday, and I have built a successful business.

In other words, I'm no dummy.

However, the only thing I understand about the dawn of FM radio is that it was invented by Edwin Howard Armstrong in the 1930s, and that he financed the construction of the first station in 1937. Everything else is a complete blur of words like *modulation*, *baseband*, *pre-emphasis*, and *triangular spectral distribution*.

Magic 8 Ball

Is John McCain too old to be president?
You may rely on it.

You

According to Census Department estimates for July 1, 2007, there are 301,621,157 people currently living in the United States—and 274,485,639 (or roughly 91 percent) of them are younger than 70.

Now, does this mean that John McCain would automatically be a bad president because he's older than 91 percent of the country? Of course not. But does it make a case that he might not be so connected to the issues of a staggeringly overwhelming part of the country? I think that it does.

By comparison, roughly 68 percent of the population is the same age or younger than Barack Obama.

What does that mean? I don't know—what does it mean to you?

Extras

Our Cruel Bodies, Ourselves

It's a fact. As we age, our bodies begin to function differently. Here's an edited list of some of the fun things we all have to look forward to (some of us sooner than later):

Lean muscle mass decreases.
Lipofuscin builds up in the
    brain and dulls memory.
Organs shrink in size.
Basal metabolism rate decreases.
Antioxidants decrease.

The ability to go into a "deep
    sleep" decreases.
Body strength, stamina,
    and reflex speeds decrease.
Lung efficiency decreases.

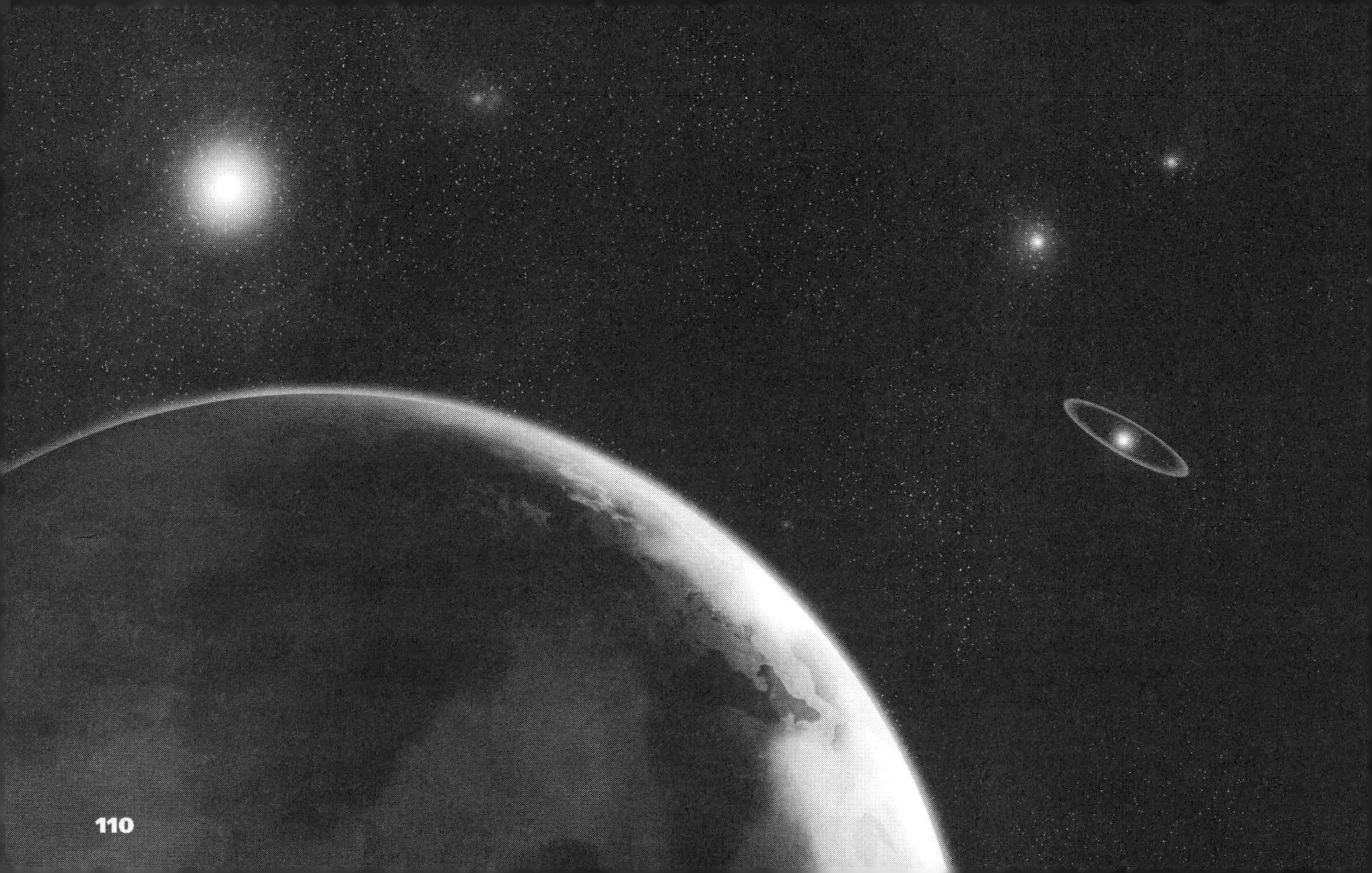

So Close

Things that are almost younger than John McCain that I wished I could have used because they could have been really funny.

Wilford Brimley
(Born 9/27/34)

Larry King
(Born 11/19/33)

Jerry Lewis
(Born 3/16/26)

Jerry Lee Lewis
(Born 9/29/35)

Rich Uncle Pennybags
(of Monopoly fame)
("Born" in 1936)

Alcatraz
(Opened as a federal
prison in April 1934)

The first Soap Box Derby
(8/19/33)

The discovery of Pluto
(1930)

Yoko Ono
(Born 2/18/33)

Bonus Section

THINGS OLDER THAN McCAIN

The War of 1812

Abe Vigoda

Fire

Stonehenge

The Spanish Inquisition

Other, non-Spanish inquisitions

Dirt

Half the things in my refrigerator

Ramses (the pharaoh, not the condom)

Most jokes about two guys walking into a bar

Money

The Wheel

Jesus

Photo Credits

About the Author

I'm 41.
I think the only word that's funnier than *pants* is *slacks*.
I don't work for Obama.
I didn't work for Hillary.
I don't hate old people.